Raintree is an imprint of Capstone Global Library Limited, a company incorporated in England and Wales having its registered office at 264 Banbury Road, Oxford, OX2 7DY – Registered company number: 6695582

www.raintree.co.uk
myorders@raintree.co.uk

Edited by Marissa Kirkman
Designed by Sarah Bennett
Original illustrations © Capstone Global Library Limited 2019
Picture research by Tracy Cummins
Production by Laura Manthe
Originated by Capstone Global Library Ltd
Printed and bound in India

ISBN 978 1 4747 6088 1
22 21 20 19 18
10 9 8 7 6 5 4 3 2 1

British Library Cataloguing in Publication Data
A full catalogue record for this book is available from the British Library.

Acknowledgements
We would like to thank the following for permission to reproduce photographs: Alamy: Juniors Bildarchiv GmbH, 9; Capstone Studio: Karon Dubke, 5, 7, 13, 16; iStockphoto: tc397, 18; Shutterstock: anusorn2005, Cover, bluehand, 3, Chaikom, 7 Inset, chonlasub woravichan, 21 Top, Cultura Motion, 8, ekmelica, Design Element, julie deshaies, 23, Kateryna Dyellalova, 21 Middle Right, Mike Richter, 20, Mirko Rosenau, 11, Napat, Back Cover, 24, PAUL ATKINSON, 21 Middle Left, Pavel Pomoleyko, 17, Podolnaya Elena, 21 Bottom, Steve Bower, 15, UMA SEN, 10, Vojce, 4, 19; SuperStock: NHPA, 12.

Every effort has been made to contact copyright holders of material reproduced in this book. Any omissions will be rectified in subsequent printings if notice is given to the publisher.

Contents

Your new pet fish

Many people enjoy watching colourful fish swim around in tanks. Fish make great pets. But you must learn a few things about them before setting up your own tank.

You can buy fish at pet shops. Ask a member of staff about which types of fish can live together peacefully.

FACT

Some fish live in fresh water. Others live in salt water. Talk to your family about which type of fish will make the best pet for you.

These colourful fish live in salt water.

Things you will need

You will need to set up an **aquarium** for your fish before bringing them home. Most fish tanks need a heater and a **filter**. These items keep the water warm and clean. You will need gravel for the bottom of the tank.

You will also need food for your fish. You can buy all the equipment you need at a pet shop. Don't forget a small net to safely move your fish in and out of the tank.

aquarium glass tank full of water where pet fish are kept

filter tool that cleans water as it passes through it

oxygen colourless gas that people and animals breathe; humans and animals need oxygen to live

Bringing your fish home

Pet shops place fish in plastic bags with water. Float your fish inside of these plastic bags in your aquarium. This helps the fish get used to the water **temperature** in the tank. Use a small net to move the fish. Do not mix the shop's water into your tank.

Protect your fish from other pets. Cats may try to hunt fish. Some fish will also fight with other fish.

FACT

Your fish may lose some of its colour on the way home. Its normal colour will return as it adjusts to its new home.

temperature measure of how hot or cold something is

Feeding your fish

Fish food looks like small flakes. Sprinkle the food into the water two or three times a day. How much food depends on the number and size of your fish. Watch the clock. It should take your fish between two and five minutes to eat.

Feeding too much or too little food can make your fish sick. You must give the right amount of food and stick to a **schedule**.

FACT
Some types of fish eat frozen food such as **krill**. Other fish eat live food called brine shrimp.

brine shrimp

schedule plan for when things will happen

krill small, shrimp-like animal

Cleaning your aquarium

Clean your aquarium once a week. Use a sponge to keep the glass clean. Never use soap because it will kill your fish. You can use a **siphon** hose to clean the bottom of the tank.

Add clean water when you have finished. It should be the same temperature as the water left in the tank.

siphon

siphon tube that draws water upwards

Keeping your fish healthy

Watch your fish for signs that they are unwell. Fish that are unwell may stop eating, move slowly or get white spots.

You can treat the tank water with medicine. Staff at the pet shop can help you decide what type you need. Follow the directions carefully. Too much medicine can also hurt your pets.

FACT

Most **vets** do not treat fish. Staff at the pet shop or an online search may help you find a vet who can help.

vet doctor trained to take care of animals

fungus

Life with a fish

Place the tank away from windows and direct sunlight. Fish need times of both light and darkness. Turn off the tank light each night. Turn it back on each morning.

Add some **decorations** to your tank. Plants, castles or small ships make a tank look interesting. They also provide fish with spaces to swim through or hide in.

FACT

Large fish can be strong swimmers. A hood for the tank can stop them jumping out.

decoration objects in a fish tank that provide interest and shelter for your fish

Your fish through the years

Some types of fish live much longer than others. Some fish may only live for two years. Others can live for up to 20 years.

Make sure your tank is big enough for all your fish. Some fish grow very large over time. Keep your fish happy by making sure they have food and a clean tank.

An adult fish needs a tank about 7 to 12 times its own length.

Fish body language

You can tell a lot about a fish from the way it moves. Sick fish often swim on their sides. Scared fish may hide behind plants and other objects in the tank. A fish will usually stay in one place when it sleeps. It may still move its fins though.

Types of fish

Freshwater fish:

- goldfish
- gourami
- tetra.

gourami

tetra

angelfish

tang

Tropical fish:

- angelfish
- clownfish
- tang.

Glossary

aquarium glass tank full of water where pet fish are kept

decoration objects in a fish tank that provide interest and shelter for your fish

filter tool that cleans water as it passes through it

krill small, shrimp-like animal

oxygen colourless gas that people and animals breathe; humans and animals need oxygen to live

schedule plan for when things will happen

siphon tube that draws water upwards

temperature measure of how hot or cold something is

vet doctor trained to take care of animals

Find out more

Books

Fantastic Fish (Extreme Animals), Isabel Thomas (Raintree, 2012)

Fish (Animal Classifications), Angela Royston (Raintree, 2015)

Fish (DK Eyewitness Books), Steve Parker (DK Publishing, 2005)

Goldie's Guide to Caring for Your Goldfish (Pets' Guides), Anita Ganeri (Raintree, 2014)

Superstar Fish (Animal Superstars), Louise Spilsbury (Raintree, 2018)

Websites

Find out more about pet care at:
www.dkfindout.com/uk/animals-and-nature/pet-care

Learn more about all sorts of animals and how to take care of them at:
young.rspca.org.uk/kids/animals

Comprehension questions

1. Why do you need to float the plastic bag with your new fish inside of it at the top of your tank?

2. What are some of the ways in which you can keep the aquarium clean for your fish?

3. What should you do if your fish are unwell?

Index